Get Fit!

by Vaishali Batra

OXFORD
UNIVERSITY PRESS
AUSTRALIA & NEW ZEALAND

How can we get fit? There are lots of things we can do.

We can go up to the treetops.

We can skip down from
the hill.

It is good for us to be fit.
We feel well and strong.

He is on a trail with his dog.

She jogs some laps.

We hang on the bars.

We like to get fit in the morning.

She is on foot and he scoots. This will keep us fit, too.

We like to get fit at lunch.

We run on the spot,
then hop and jump.

We can skip to keep fit, too.

We like to swim to get fit.

We swim laps at the pool.

We come to train at a sport to get fit.

We run and shoot for the target.

She kicks a goal!

Helping can get us fit, too.

He scrubs the dishes.

She sweeps the bricks.

How do you plan to get fit?